Preaching To The Chickens

The story of young John Lewis

JABARI ASIM

illustrated by **E.B. LEWIS**

Nancy Paulsen Books

NANCY PAULSEN BOOKS

an imprint of Penguin Random House LLC

375 Hudson Street

New York, NY 10014

Library of Congress Cataloging-in-Publication Data

Names: Asim, Jabari, 1962–, author. | Lewis, Earl B., illustrator.

Title: Preaching to the chickens / Jabari Asim ; illustrated by E. B. Lewis.

Description: New York : Nancy Paulsen Books, [2016]

Identifiers: LCCN 2015048281 | ISBN 9780399168567 (hardback)

Subjects: LCSH: Lewis, John, 1940 February 21—Childhood and youth—Juvenile literature. | African
American civil rights workers—Religious life—Juvenile literature. | African American boys—Alabama—
Biography—Juvenile literature. | Chickens—Juvenile literature. | Preaching—Juvenile literature. | Rural
children—Alabama—Juvenile literature. | Legislators—United States—Biography—Juvenile literature. |
African American legislators—Biography—Juvenile literature. | Alabama—Rural conditions—20th cen-
tury—Juvenile literature. | Christian biography—United States—Juvenile literature. | BISAC: JUVENILE
NONFICTION / Biography & Autobiography / Social Activists. | JUVENILE NONFICTION / People & Places
/ United States / African American. | JUVENILE NONFICTION / History / United States / 20th Century.

Classification: LCC E840.8.L43 A75 2016 | DDC 328.73/092 [B]—dc23

LC record available at https://lccn.loc.gov/2015048281

Manufactured in China by RR Donnelley Asia Printing Solutions Ltd.

ISBN 9780399168567

10 9 8 7 6 5 4 3

Design by Annie Ericsson.

Text set in Fiesole Text Bold.

The art was done in watercolor and gouache.

To the GrandGirls, Genzya and Amandla—J.A.

To John Lewis and the soldiers who fought for civil rights, and to my adopted school, Plantersville Elementary School, in South Carolina—E.B.L.

Little John Lewis loved the spring. He loved it not only because it was the time when the whole planet came alive, but also because it was the season of the chicks. Winter was too cold to bring them safely into the world, and summer was too hot. Spring was just right.

Everyone on the farm had work to do. "Work and put your trust in God," John's mama liked to say, "and God's gonna take care of his children."

Trusting in God was easy. Work was a harder bargain. There was just so much to do on a huge farm in southern Alabama. Every March, John's father hitched the plow to his stubborn old mule. "Giddyup!" he'd shout, and together they'd break new ground, carving lines in the earth. In the fall, after months of planting, weeding, and tending, the cotton would be ready for picking.

John's mother cooked the family meals from vegetables she grew—collards, tomatoes, sweet potatoes—and other goodies. She cleaned the family's clothes in a big iron pot, stirring them in the boiling water and washing them with homemade soap before hanging them on the line to dry.

Yes, Lord, plenty of work on a farm.

John was excited to be put in charge of the chickens. There were about sixty of them: Rhode Island Reds. Strong-winged bantams. Dominiques with gray stripes as dull as dishwater and legs as yellow as daisies. John loved to see them flutter and strut and flap their wings.

Every day, John got up early and fed them dried corn just shelled from the cob, then lined their nests with fresh straw.

"Cluck, cluck, cluck," the chickens said.

John knew they meant "thank you."

In a soft voice, John would say to them,
"Enjoy this day that God has given us."
The chickens, looking straight at him,
seemed to understand.

As much as John loved spring, he loved church even more. On Sundays, the whole family headed to services. John and his brothers were dressed in slacks and crisp white shirts, his sisters in neat dresses. Outside the church, friends and relatives greeted each other with big smiles.

Inside, voices joined in song. John often listened to gospel and country music on the radio. He enjoyed it, but he found his favorite music of all in church: plain voices praising God without any instruments at all.

Amazing Grace! How sweet the sound
That saved a wretch like me.
I once was lost, but now am found,
Was blind, but now I see.

As the worshippers clapped and sang, John felt the Holy Spirit rocking the room. It reminded him of the peace he felt when he roused the chickens from slumber and led them into the light of a brand-new day.

Like the ministers he heard in church, John wanted to preach, so he gathered his chickens in the yard.

John stretched his arms above his flock and let the words pour forth. The chickens nodded and dipped their beaks as if they agreed. They swayed to the rhythm of his voice.

John's brothers and sisters couldn't tell one bird from another. John knew every one, and he had a line of verse for each of them.

"Blessed are the peacemakers," he'd say when they fought over their morning meal.

"Blessed are those who hunger and thirst for righteousness," he would tell a hen who didn't want to share, "for they shall be satisfied."

One day, the rolling store man stopped by to make a trade. His truck was packed with flour, sugar, cooking oil, and bolts of cloth in bright colors. "I've got plenty of good things," he said to John's mom and dad. "I'll give them to you for a healthy hen."

But John did not want to part with any of his chickens, and he knew they wanted to stay with him. He convinced his parents there were other things to trade, like eggs and seeds. The chickens stayed on the farm, and John learned to speak up for those who can't speak for themselves.

When the hen called Big Belle fell into the well and got stuck, John was determined to save her. He filled a basket with bread crumbs, and when he lowered it down, she climbed in and was pulled to safety.

"God makes miracles every day," John preached. "When you're down, he lifts you up. Sister Big Belle, I believe you know what I mean."

"Cluck, cluck, cluck," Big Belle replied. John knew she meant "amen."

John even baptized the chicks, bathing them in water from an old syrup can. But Li'l Pullet had stayed under too long and appeared to have drowned. John prayed over her and laid her in the sun. After a while, she began to breathe again and soon was up on her feet.

"He can heal the sick," John declared, "and raise the dead. Li'l Pullet, can I get a witness?"

"Peep, peep, peep," said Li'l Pullet.
John knew she meant "amen."

John loved to tell the hens and chicks the Good News. While he fed and watered them, he spoke about the value of hard work and patience. With faith and hope, he said, a bountiful harvest was sure to come.

John's henhouse sermons became so regular that his brothers and sisters took to calling him Preacher. He didn't mind. He knew that someday he'd speak before thousands. He hoped that his words would stir people's souls and move them to action. For now, though, he had his own church right here among the pine trees and rolling hills of southern Alabama. Morning would find him in his usual place, preaching to the chickens.

Author's Note

I've always been an enthusiastic admirer of John Lewis. I knew of his brave participation as an original member of the Freedom Riders, Americans who in 1961 rode buses into the Deep South to protest the segregation of black and white travelers, who were forced to sit on separate benches and drink from separate fountains. I was aware that he had been chairman of the Student Nonviolent Coordinating Committee (SNCC, pronounced "snick"), a group of young people who used civil disobedience to work toward full equality for all. I knew that he had been the youngest member of the "Big Six," black leaders who led the March on Washington for Jobs and Freedom in 1963, the largest public demonstration in American history at that time. I knew that in 1965 he stood with the Rev. Hosea Williams at the front of the line when troopers attacked unarmed demonstrators on the Edmund Pettus Bridge in Selma, Alabama.

I learned even more about Lewis when I read *Walking with the Wind*, his extraordinary memoir. In it, he wrote, "I never really saw myself as a leader in the traditional sense of the word. I saw myself as a participator, an activist, a doer."

Not long after I read the book, I met Lewis when I had the great privilege of introducing him at the National Book Festival on the National Mall. I found myself drawn to the passages in his memoir in which he described his childhood in Pike County, Alabama. As a young boy he dreamed of being a preacher, moving crowds to action with the power of his sermons. But he was a doer even then, and instead of just dreaming, he practiced with a captive audience: the chickens on his family farm. "I preached to my birds just about every night," he wrote. "They would sit very quietly, some slightly moving their heads back and forth, mesmerized, I guess, by the sound of my voice. I could imagine that they were my congregation. And me, I was a preacher."

I relied on Lewis's recollections when fashioning this story, especially his memories of Li'l Pullet and Big Belle. I hope readers will find the resulting tale as mesmerizing as those chickens found young John Lewis long ago.